NEW YORK JETS

LUKE HANLON

WWW.APEXEDITIONS.COM

Copyright © 2025 by Apex Editions, Mendota Heights, MN 55120. All rights reserved. No part of this book may be reproduced or utilized in any form or by any means without written permission from the publisher.

Apex is distributed by North Star Editions:
sales@northstareditions.com | 888-417-0195

Produced for Apex by Red Line Editorial.

Photographs ©: Tom DiPace/AP Images, cover, 1; Lauren Bacho/AP Images, 4–5; John Minchillo/AP Images, 6–7; Bob Campbell/San Francisco Chronicle/AP Images, 8–9; Focus On Sport/Getty Images Sport/Getty Images, 10–11, 26–27; David Durochik/AP Images, 12–13; Paul Spinelli/AP Images, 14–15, 58–59; Chuck Burton/AP Images, 16–17; Tony Tomsic/AP Images, 19, 22–23, 57; Vernon Biever/AP Images, 20–21; Al Messerschmidt/AP Images, 24–25; Tom Hauck/Allsport/Getty Images Sport/Getty Images, 28–29; Stephen Dunn/Getty Images Sport/Getty Images, 30–31; Al Pereira/Getty Images Sport/Getty Images, 32–33, 42–43, 47; Stephen Pond/Getty Images Sport/Getty Images, 34–35; Chuck Solomon/AP Images, 37; Bernstein Associates/Getty Images Sport/Getty Images, 38–39; George Gojkovich/Getty Images Sport/Getty Images, 40–41; Cooper Neill/Getty Images Sport/Getty Images, 44–45; Shutterstock Images, 48–49; Andy Lyons/Allsport/Getty Images Sport/Getty Images, 50–51; Al Pereira/New York Jets/Getty Images Sport/Getty Images, 52–53; Al Bello/Getty Images Sport/Getty Images, 54–55

Library of Congress Control Number: 2024939373

ISBN
979-8-89250-158-3 (hardcover)
979-8-89250-175-0 (paperback)
979-8-89250-299-3 (ebook pdf)
979-8-89250-192-7 (hosted ebook)

Printed in the United States of America
Mankato, MN
012025

NOTE TO PARENTS AND EDUCATORS

Apex books are designed to build literacy skills in striving readers. Exciting, high-interest content attracts and holds readers' attention. The text is carefully leveled to allow students to achieve success quickly.

TABLE OF CONTENTS

CHAPTER 1
J-E-T-S, JETS, JETS, JETS! 4

CHAPTER 2
EARLY HISTORY 8

PLAYER SPOTLIGHT
JOE NAMATH 18

CHAPTER 3
LEGENDS 20

CHAPTER 4
RECENT HISTORY 28

PLAYER SPOTLIGHT
MARK GASTINEAU 36

CHAPTER 5
MODERN STARS 38

PLAYER SPOTLIGHT
CURTIS MARTIN 46

CHAPTER 6
TEAM TRIVIA 48

TEAM RECORDS • 56
TIMELINE • 58
COMPREHENSION QUESTIONS • 60
GLOSSARY • 62
TO LEARN MORE • 63
ABOUT THE AUTHOR • 63
INDEX • 64

CHAPTER 1

J-E-T-S, JETS, JETS, JETS!

It's a beautiful Sunday afternoon. New York Jets fans fill the stadium. The crowd is a sea of green. The Jets have several exciting young players. The fans are ready to cheer them on.

Jets fans clap and shout as the players run onto the field.

Sauce Gardner returns an interception during a 2022 game against the Buffalo Bills.

The Jets defense needs a big stop. The fans get louder. Cornerback Sauce Gardner grabs an interception. The crowd goes wild. Now the offense has great field position. A few plays later, New York scores a touchdown. It's a good day to be a Jets fan.

SPELL IT OUT

A Jets tradition started in 1979. A fan in the upper deck wanted to fire up the crowd. He yelled, "J-E-T-S, Jets, Jets, Jets!" The chant caught on. Jets fans have yelled it ever since.

CHAPTER 2

EARLY HISTORY

The Jets played their first game in 1960. Back then, they were called the Titans. The Titans played in the AFL. This league was separate from the NFL. In 1963, new owners bought the Titans. They changed the team's name to the Jets.

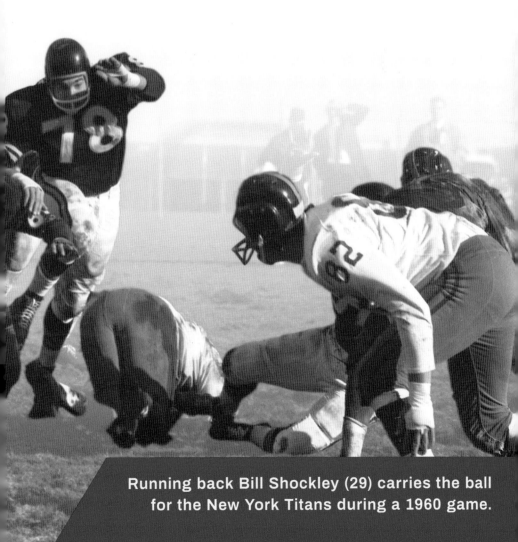

Running back Bill Shockley (29) carries the ball for the New York Titans during a 1960 game.

Running back Emerson Boozer (32) looks for a running lane during the Super Bowl.

New York didn't have much success at first. But that changed in 1968. Behind quarterback Joe Namath, the Jets won the AFL title. The win sent them to the Super Bowl. They faced the Baltimore Colts. Most people expected the Colts to win easily. But New York pulled off a huge upset. The Jets were Super Bowl champions!

FAMILIAR FOE

Weeb Ewbank led the Baltimore Colts to two NFL titles. He took over as the Jets' head coach in 1963. Ewbank later led the Jets to a Super Bowl win against his old team.

The Jets kept rolling after the Super Bowl win. In 1969, they won their division again. However, they fell short in the playoffs.

In 1970, the AFL became part of the NFL. The Jets struggled in their new league. They went 11 years without a winning record.

WHAT'S IN A NAME?

In 1964, the Jets started playing at Shea Stadium. The stadium sat near two busy airports. So, calling the team the Jets was a natural fit. The Jets shared the stadium. The New York Mets baseball team played there, too.

Defensive end Gerry Philbin (81) tries to block a pass during a 1969 game against the Kansas City Chiefs.

The Jets put together a winning season in 1981. However, they lost their first playoff game. In 1982, New York returned to the playoffs. This time, the Jets blew out the Cincinnati Bengals in the first round. Then they beat the Los Angeles Raiders. Their run ended with a loss in the conference title game.

GOOD TO BE BACK

A strike shortened the 1982 season. Two months passed between the Jets' second and third games. Their first game back was against the Baltimore Colts. The Jets won 37–0.

Freeman McNeil (24) carries the ball during a playoff game against the Raiders.

In 1986, the Jets looked like Super Bowl contenders. They started the season 10–1. But then they lost their last five games. New York still squeaked into the playoffs. In the second round, the Jets lost a heartbreaker. The Cleveland Browns beat them 23–20 in double overtime.

The Jets saw more drama in 1991. They entered the last week of the season 7–8. New York beat the Miami Dolphins in overtime. That win secured a spot in the playoffs.

Jets players celebrate an overtime victory over the Dolphins in 1991.

PLAYER SPOTLIGHT

JOE NAMATH

Joe Namath was a perfect fit in New York. The quarterback embraced the big city. And fans loved the way he played. In 1967, "Broadway Joe" became the first player to throw for more than 4,000 yards in a season.

Namath's stardom took off in the 1968 season. Days before the Super Bowl, he guaranteed the Jets would win. Few people believed him. But Namath delivered. The Jets won 16–7. Namath also earned the game's Most Valuable Player (MVP) Award.

> **JOE NAMATH THREW 170 TOUCHDOWN PASSES IN HIS 12 YEARS WITH THE JETS.**

CHAPTER 3

LEGENDS

Joe Namath started playing for the Jets in 1965. He threw 11 touchdown passes to Don Maynard that season. Maynard continued to be Namath's favorite target for years. No one in Jets history has more receiving yards than Maynard.

Don Maynard scored 88 touchdowns in his 13 seasons with New York.

The Jets had several other weapons in the 1960s. Running back Matt Snell won the AFL Rookie of the Year Award in 1964. In 1967, running back Emerson Boozer led the AFL in touchdowns. That same year, receiver George Sauer led the league in catches.

MR. CONSISTENT

Winston Hill started his pro career in 1963. The offensive lineman played in 195 straight games. And he started 174 straight. Both are team records. Hill spent 14 years with New York. He made the Pro Bowl in eight of those seasons.

Matt Snell (41) scored New York's only touchdown in the Super Bowl.

Wesley Walker posted more than 8,300 receiving yards in his career.

New York had a great defense in the late 1960s. Defensive lineman Gerry Philbin racked up dozens of sacks. Philbin's pass rushing helped linebacker Larry Grantham. He recorded 24 interceptions with the Jets.

BIG-PLAY RECEIVER

Wesley Walker didn't catch a ton of passes. But when he did, they often went for huge gains. In 1978, he led the NFL with 1,169 receiving yards. Walker remained a deep threat for 13 seasons.

Joe Klecko (73) finished his career with 78 sacks.

In the 1980s, the Jets had another strong group of defenders. Defensive lineman Joe Klecko had 20.5 sacks in 1981. That earned him the Defensive Player of the Year Award. Mark Gastineau played on the opposite end of the line. In 1983, he led the league with 19 sacks. Then, in 1984, he recorded 22. That set an NFL record.

NEW YORK SACK EXCHANGE

New York City is home to a famous business center. It's called the New York Stock Exchange. In the 1980s, the Jets took down quarterbacks with ease. So, the team's defense became known as the "New York Sack Exchange."

CHAPTER 4

RECENT HISTORY

The Jets found more success in 1998. They won their division for the first time since 1969. Then they made it all the way to the conference title game. New York took a 10–0 lead. But the Denver Broncos charged back. The Jets lost a tough one, 23–10.

Keyshawn Johnson (19) sprints down the field during a playoff game against the Broncos.

Chad Pennington (10) fires a pass during a playoff game against the Chargers.

New York hired Herm Edwards in 2001. The new head coach led the Jets to the playoffs in his first year. They made it twice more in the next three years. In the 2004 season, the Jets won a playoff thriller in overtime. But a down year followed in 2005. After that, the Jets fired Edwards.

YOU PLAY TO WIN THE GAME

In 2002, the Jets got off to a rough start. Reporters asked Herm Edwards about it. He said, "You play to win the game!" He repeated it several times. His speech fired up the team. The Jets won seven of their last nine games. They even won their division.

The Jets hired a new coach in 2009. Rex Ryan turned the team's defense into a powerhouse. In Ryan's first season, New York won two road playoff games. In 2010, the Jets won two more playoff games on the road. But in both seasons, they fell short in the conference title game.

FAMILY TIES

Rex Ryan wasn't the first member of his family to coach for the Jets. His dad, Buddy Ryan, coached New York's linebackers from 1968 to 1975. Buddy was known for building excellent defenses.

Shonn Greene (23) ran for 135 yards and a touchdown during a playoff win over the Cincinnati Bengals.

The Jets struggled after 2010. Coaches came and went. None were able to find success. The team went through a long playoff drought. The 2015 season was a bright spot. New York won 10 games that year. Even so, that wasn't enough to make the playoffs.

TOUGH START

New York traded for Aaron Rodgers in 2023. The Jets hoped the superstar quarterback could lead the team to the Super Bowl. However, Rodgers played only four snaps that season. He got hurt during his first game with the Jets.

Wide receiver Brandon Marshall made the Pro Bowl in 2015.

PLAYER SPOTLIGHT

MARK GASTINEAU

These days, defensive players often celebrate good plays. Some players even have specific dances they do after sacks. Mark Gastineau was one of the first players to celebrate sacks. And he had plenty of chances to do it. He led the NFL in sacks two years in a row.

Gastineau jumped off the line in a flash. His speed helped him blow by offensive linemen. Gastineau spent his entire 10-year career with the Jets. In that time, he recorded 107.5 sacks. No other Jets player has more than 78.

> **MARK GASTINEAU MADE THE PRO BOWL FIVE YEARS IN A ROW FROM 1981 TO 1985.**

CHAPTER 5

MODERN STARS

Wide receiver Al Toon wanted to improve his footwork. So, he took ballet classes. The classes paid off. Toon used his graceful skill to get open. Starting in 1986, he led the Jets in catches for six straight seasons.

Al Toon led the NFL with 93 catches in 1988.

Curtis Martin led the Jets offense for eight seasons. The running back ran for at least 1,000 yards seven times. Martin got help from Kevin Mawae. The center cleared huge running lanes. Mawae played during all seven of Martin's 1,000-yard seasons.

FIRST-ROUND FINDS

The Jets had two picks in the first round of the 2006 draft. They selected D'Brickashaw Ferguson and Nick Mangold. Both offensive linemen made multiple Pro Bowls. And they anchored the Jets offensive line for years.

Kevin Mawae (68) was voted into the Pro Football Hall of Fame in 2019.

The Jets defense had several stars in the 2000s. Defensive lineman Shaun Ellis made big hits on quarterbacks. But no star shined brighter than Darrelle Revis. The defensive back pulled down six interceptions in 2009. Then he had zero in 2010. That's because quarterbacks were afraid to throw toward him.

WORTH THE HYPE

The Jets drafted Quinnen Williams in 2019. The defensive lineman quickly started to dominate. Williams became known for his massive frame. He used it to stuff running lanes. He also used his quickness to rush the passer.

Darrelle Revis returns an interception for a touchdown during a 2009 game against the Carolina Panthers.

The Jets drafted defensive back Sauce Gardner in 2022. As a rookie, he broke up 20 pass attempts. That led the NFL. Gardner earned the Defensive Rookie of the Year Award.

New York also drafted receiver Garrett Wilson in 2022. He topped 1,100 receiving yards in his first season. He won the Offensive Rookie of the Year Award. Wilson and Gardner became the third pair of teammates to win these awards.

Garrett Wilson recorded more than 2,100 receiving yards in his first two seasons.

PLAYER SPOTLIGHT

CURTIS MARTIN

Curtis Martin's greatest skill may have been his durability. The running back took lots of hits. Yet he rarely missed games. That's how he ran for more than 10,000 yards during eight seasons with the Jets.

Martin's toughness was on full display in 2004. He hurt his knee early in the season. But he played through the pain. Martin finished the year with 1,697 rushing yards. That led the NFL.

> **CURTIS MARTIN HAD SEVEN STRAIGHT 1,000-YARD SEASONS WITH THE JETS.**

CHAPTER 6

TEAM TRIVIA

The Jets do not actually play in New York. Their home games are in East Rutherford, New Jersey. The Jets have played in their current stadium since 2010. They share the building with the New York Giants.

The Jets' stadium can hold more than 82,000 fans.

Wayne Chrebet grew up in New Jersey. The wide receiver played college football in New York. In 1995, he went undrafted. But the Jets signed Chrebet after a tryout. He went on to have an 11-year career with New York. Jets fans loved the underdog wide receiver.

BACK IN BLACK

The Jets' jerseys have not changed much since 1963. They always feature green and white. In 2019, the team added black jerseys. Then in 2022, New York added black helmets as well.

Wayne Chrebet recorded more than 7,300 receiving yards during his career.

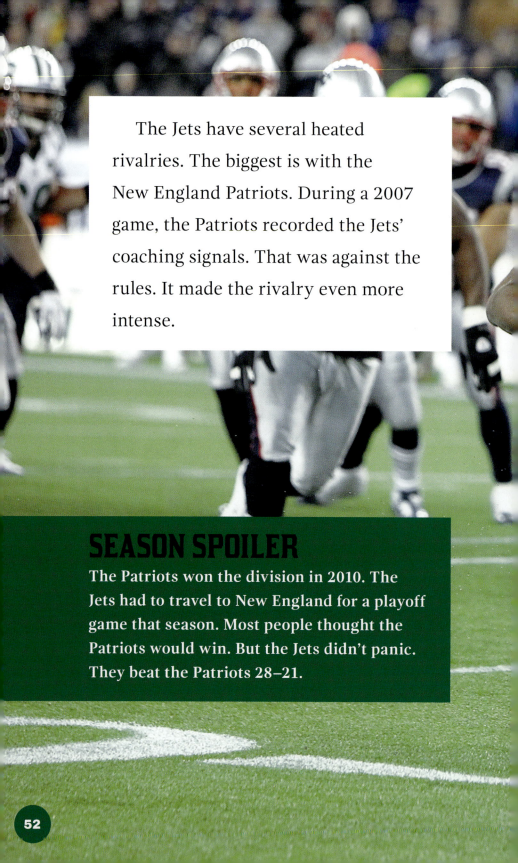

The Jets have several heated rivalries. The biggest is with the New England Patriots. During a 2007 game, the Patriots recorded the Jets' coaching signals. That was against the rules. It made the rivalry even more intense.

SEASON SPOILER

The Patriots won the division in 2010. The Jets had to travel to New England for a playoff game that season. Most people thought the Patriots would win. But the Jets didn't panic. They beat the Patriots 28–21.

Wide receiver Braylon Edwards (17) makes his way into the end zone during a playoff game against the Patriots.

Fireman Ed cheers on his team during a game in 2010.

Jets fan Ed Anzalone worked as a firefighter. He started going to Jets games in the 1970s. At games, Anzalone wears a firefighter helmet with the Jets logo on it. The team's fans know him as "Fireman Ed."

THRILLING END

One of New York's most exciting games happened in 2023. The Jets hosted the Buffalo Bills. The game was tied after four quarters. In overtime, the Jets received a punt. Rookie Xavier Gipson returned it for a touchdown. The Jets won the game.

TEAM RECORDS

All-Time Passing Yards: 27,057
Joe Namath (1965–76)

All-Time Touchdown Passes: 170
Joe Namath (1965–76)

All-Time Rushing Yards: 10,302
Curtis Martin (1998–2005)

All-Time Receiving Yards: 11,732
Don Maynard (1960–72)

All-Time Touchdowns: 88
Don Maynard (1960–72)

All-Time Scoring: 1,470
Pat Leahy (1974–91)

All-Time Interceptions: 34
Bill Baird (1963–69)

All-Time Sacks: 107.5*
Mark Gastineau (1979–88)

All-Time Coaching Wins: 71
Weeb Ewbank (1963–73)

Super Bowl Titles: 1
(1968)

* Sacks were not an official statistic until 1982. However, researchers have studied old games to determine sacks dating back to 1960.

All statistics are accurate through 2023.

TIMELINE

1960 — The Titans of New York play their first AFL season.

1963 — The Titans change their name to the New York Jets.

1968 — The Jets win the AFL title and then upset the Baltimore Colts to win the Super Bowl.

1970 — The Jets play their first NFL season.

1984 — Mark Gastineau sets a record for most sacks in a season.

1998 — The Jets win their division for the first time since 1969 and make a trip to the conference title game.

2002 — After starting 2–5, the Jets finish the season 9–7 and win their division.

2004 — Curtis Martin runs for 1,697 yards and wins the NFL rushing title.

2010 — Head coach Rex Ryan leads the Jets to the conference title game for the second season in a row.

2023 — The Jets trade for quarterback Aaron Rodgers, who gets hurt in his first game with the team.

COMPREHENSION QUESTIONS

Write your answers on a separate piece of paper.

1. Write a paragraph that explains the main ideas of Chapter 2.

2. Who do you think was the greatest player in Jets history? Why?

3. Who guaranteed the Jets would win the Super Bowl?

    A. Weeb Ewbank
    B. Joe Namath
    C. Don Maynard

4. Why was the Jets' defensive line called the "New York Sack Exchange" in the 1980s?

    A. They had trouble stopping the run.
    B. They made a lot of money.
    C. They often tackled the quarterback.

5. What does **contenders** mean in this book?

*In 1986, the Jets looked like Super Bowl **contenders**. They started the season 10–1.*

    A. a young team without many good players
    B. a team that does not finish a full season
    C. a team with a good chance of winning a title

6. What does **durability** mean in this book?

*Curtis Martin's greatest skill may have been his **durability**. The running back took lots of hits. Yet he rarely missed games.*

    A. the ability to miss games
    B. the ability to run quickly
    C. the ability to stay healthy

Answer key on page 64.

GLOSSARY

conference
A group of teams that make up part of a sports league.

division
In the NFL, a group of teams that make up part of a conference.

draft
A system that lets teams select new players coming into the league.

interception
A pass that is caught by a defensive player.

rookie
An athlete in his or her first year as a professional player.

sacks
Plays that happen when a defender tackles the quarterback before he can throw the ball.

snaps
Backward passes that start plays. A snap usually goes from the center to the quarterback.

strike
When people stop working as a way to demand better pay or better working conditions.

tradition
A way of doing something that is passed down over many years.

upset
When a team wins a game that it was expected to lose.

TO LEARN MORE

BOOKS

Anderson, Josh. *New York Jets*. Mankato, MN: The Child's World, 2022.

Blue, Tyler. *Stars of the NFL*. New York: Abbeville Press, 2023.

Coleman, Ted. *New York Jets All-Time Greats*. Mendota Heights, MN: Press Box Books, 2022.

ONLINE RESOURCES

Visit **www.apexeditions.com** to find links and resources related to this title.

ABOUT THE AUTHOR

Luke Hanlon is a sportswriter, editor, and author based in Minneapolis. He watches NFL games all day on Sundays during the fall.

INDEX

Boozer, Emerson, 22

Chrebet, Wayne, 50

Edwards, Herm, 31
Ellis, Shaun, 42
Ewbank, Weeb, 11

Ferguson,
 D'Brickashaw, 40

Gardner, Sauce, 7, 44
Gastineau, Mark, 27, 36
Grantham, Larry, 25

Hill, Winston, 22

Klecko, Joe, 27

Mangold, Nick, 40
Martin, Curtis, 40, 46
Mawae, Kevin, 40
Maynard, Don, 20

Namath, Joe, 11, 18, 20

Philbin, Gerry, 25

Revis, Darrelle, 42
Rodgers, Aaron, 34
Ryan, Rex, 32

Sauer, George, 22
Snell, Matt, 22

Toon, Al, 38

Walker, Wesley, 25
Williams, Quinnen, 42
Wilson, Garrett, 44

ANSWER KEY:
1. Answers will vary; 2. Answers will vary; 3. B; 4. C; 5. C; 6. C